VALBONA B VOCA

WHISPERS OF THE HEART

FROM SHADOWS TO LIGHT

TRANSFORMATIONAL POEMS OF LOVE, SPIRITUAL AWAKENING AND FAITH

BLUEROSE PUBLISHERS
India | U.K.

For permissions requests or inquiries regarding this publication,
please contact:

BLUEROSE PUBLISHERS
www.BlueRoseONE.com
info@bluerosepublishers.com
+91 8882 898 898
+4407342408967

ISBN: 978-93-6452-324-0

Cover design: Shivani
Typesetting: Sagar

First Edition: September 2024

Contents

1.

Whispers of the Heart

A glowing heart fell from the stars above,
To a world of shadows, far from love.
She landed in fog, thick as night,
In air too thin for her soul's bright light.

In a world where her brilliance outshone the norm,
And shadows conspired to silence her storm,
This heart, too pure for Earth's deceitful chains,
Realised early on, that she must break free, ascend and claim.

Longing for home, where stars sing her name,
Yet knowing her mission: Earth's light to reclaim.
She whispered her hope through the night's endless sway,
Pledging to shine and to keep darkness at bay.

I'm here to illuminate the deepest dark,
To spread love's warmth, to make my mark.
No storm, no fire, nor beast so wild,
Can dim my light—I am the chosen child.

Agonies, unimagined, struck her core,
Loneliness whispered at her heart's door.
Yet, softly she murmured, "You are the light,
Rise above shadows, take flight, ignite.

Her heart-built shields, like castles of stone,
Turning soft whispers into a powerful tone.
She aimed for rainbows, high in the sky,
To blaze her light where shadows lie.

The soul never failed, whispers kept her alive,
Her mission was imprinted within, and her spirit thrived.
To spread her light, to heal and ignite,
A path to awaken human insight.

2.

Quest for Light

My spirit's lamp shattered and torn,
Why drown in tears, heart heavy and worn?
Fear, a phantom stalking the night,
As spring's dawn meets solemn plight.

Spare me, life, from endless pain,
Though tears flow, my heart refrains,
Strength falters in shadows' cruel play,
Yet yearning for light leads the way.

Rise, spirit, from fear's dark shroud,
Despite loneliness, truth shall be loud,
Chase the sun's embrace, let warmth ignite,
Love's tender grace, from realms so bright.

In the fractured lamp of my spirit's plight,
Why linger in tears, through endless nights?
Fear haunts like a phantom, soul in its hold,
But in spring's dawn, a purpose unfolds.

Life, spare me not, yet ease this pain,
Though my eyes weep, let hope remain,
Strength may stumble in shadows' sway,
But the longing for light guides each day.

Rise high from fear's grim embrace,
Though loneliness lingers, truth will chase,
Embrace the sun's warmth, let love entwine,
A divine gift, in life's sacred design.

3.

Dreams

A dream tied with ribbons of rainbow light,
Fragrant roses and waterfalls' delight,
Beneath orange blossoms' tranquil shade,
My heart finds peace, yet trembles, afraid.

Each night you come, a signal in the storm,
Inspiring a soul to take its true form,
The song persists in its endless play,
Tears fall silently, with no words to say.

Wide Horizons invite me, they call me high,
To climb the sky, without wings to fly,
To reach for the stars, the moon's gentle face,
In the sun's warm glow, find freedom's embrace.

A cup brimming with love's tender art,
Dream, hold me close, don't let us part,
For I resist the waking's cruel blow,
In dreams' sweet refuge, I long to grow.

4.

I am Human - A symphony of being

Hold your judgments earthy creatures,
Don't spread poison, withhold your tongue
I have passion in my veins, I crave to be
I never was part of the crowd, nor do I want to be

Let me orchestrate my own tune,
Symphony of Pain, a melody so true
I yearn for life's sweet breath; I will always fight for more
Whatever it takes, I will seek a liberty that unveils my timeless
core,

Yet, I've had to learn harsh lessons, I must confess.
My soul, a wanderer through virtue's veil and sin's cobweb,
What law, what cosmic decree can chain the soul's flight?
In love's labyrinth depths, where stars ignite,

I am but a wanderer, a pilgrim of the heart,
In my wounds, beyond my scars, I play my part.
Do not weigh my spirit against morality's scale,
For in this life span, I fail and prevail.

Do not judge the thunder of my soul's echo,
When sorrow veils my smile when tears fall like rain.
In the tenderness of my heart, I find my way,
Enduring the storm's rage, embracing the night.

For, I am human, bearer of joy and pain,
A vessel of light amidst the darkest domain
In the tapestry of the divine, I trace my soul's destiny
I pray I despair, and with my voice, I ask for mercy

You might not comprehend. but do not judge me
As I am but an astral traveller, seeking the truth,
No matter the storm, no matter the price
I have to find and walk in my life's path

If I kneel before the altar of despair,
It is but to seek redemption, to breathe in hope's rare air.
For I believe in miracles, in love's transcendent grace
In the sacred dance of existence, I find my chance

Part angel, part human, in laughter and sigh,
I go across the realms of dreams, beneath the azure sky.
I am the universe within, a painting of creation's art,
Oh, I am just a human, with dreams and miracles at heart.

5.

Reflections

Amidst the whispers of my dreams,
I dive into existence's streams,
Embracing each day's fleeting grace,
In this mortal, sacred place.

I search, I probe with endless zeal,
For the elusive truths to feel.
Streets ablaze with celestial light,
Storms that dance in the dead of night.

Yet time flows on, relentless tide,
Carving paths both deep and wide.
Writing tales in eternity's scroll,
Etching deeply in my soul.

A divine signal, mysterious, bright,
Ignites my soul, guiding me right.
A spark within, a guiding light,
Steers me through the darkest night.

I know, I sense, with all my might,
That these pages shall take flight.
Unfolding meaning, deep and grand,
The fire within, I understand.

Into uncharted lands, I boldly stride,
With fear and hope, where angels might hide.
Yet relief finds me, calm and clear,
My purpose shines, dispelling fear.

A divine light calls to me,
It's pure mystic mystery.
Yet within, a spark ignites,
Showing me how to reach the stars

I know, I feel it deep inside,
These moments hold a secret guide.
The fire within my soul does blaze,
Lighting paths through life's maze.

Often to unknown dimensions, I stray,
Fear may grip and light decay,
But willpower soon comes into sight,
Destined to kindle the guiding light.

6.

Through the Veil of Despair

Ghosts of the past awaken,
Thirsting for the warmth of life,
In a body where light has dimmed,
Darkness blinds my tear-stained eyes.

The pain cuts deep like a sword,
Shadows engulf my fragile world,
Storms that drown my flickering light,
A river of sorrow floods my heart.

My song is silent, my voice is lost,
Verses unsung, trapped in my veins,
Sorrow pours through every beat,
Petals fall in the garden of my soul.

Visions haunt my restless mind,
Wounds aching for healing light,
Yet no glow at the tunnel's end,
Only an endless night remains.

I stand frozen, shaken by an inner quake,
Within walls that refuse to break.
My gaze fixed on a single point,
On a colourless wall that knows no hope.

Watching the rainbow slowly fade away,
I wonder if the stars have lost their way.
In the open sky, do the heavens still shine,
Or is it all an illusion, a mirage in time?

In the mirror, a face without expression,
A drowning silence after the storm,
A lone oasis in a desolate desert,
Starving, it dreams of rain and bloom.

Shadows of mystery tease my weary mind,
Whispers of a soul reaching for the Universe,
Hope, though faint, flickers in the ash,
Awaiting the sun to find its light at last.

Solitude wraps me in its chilling grip,
As depths of despair seem endless and deep.
Yet at the edge of darkness, a spark takes flight,
A new self emerges, reborn with radiant light.

7.

Millions of Deaths

Each time a loved one departs this realm,
A fragment of our soul is left overwhelmed.
In the quiet ache of hearts that mourn,
We die a little with each setting sun.

If a beloved one fades from our sight,
We die a little, swallowed by the night.
A piece of our spirit in grief's cold embrace,
Each heartache etches a scar on our face

When love shatters and breaks the heart's core,
A piece of us dies, forevermore.
In the twilight's wrap, where anguish dwells,
A part of our spirit silently rebels.

Whenever love betrays, and hearts are torn apart,
A piece of us departs in the same dark.
Little by little, the reaper's hand takes its toll,
Stealing the brightest fragments of the soul.

Sometimes, in the stabs of shock and pain,
Our hearts are buried, silent, in the rain.
Joy's essence was stolen, leaving only despair,
As the soul freezes beyond repair.

Life, a thief in its endless scheme,
Steals the vibrant colours from our once-bright dreams.
In the grip of shock or unbearable pain's wave,
A part of our heart is lost, forever to the grave.

Buried in grief, with no ceremony or rite,
Fragments of our joy slip into the night.
When sadness overwhelms and life's joy fades,
Death claims our bright cells in sad parades.

Across the shifting sands of time, we die bit by bit,
Each loss is a reminder of life's cruel split.
Yet, despite the fractures and pieces that fall,
We press on, surviving, through it all.

As life unfolds, we face a thousand losses,
In subtle, silent deaths where our bright spirit crosses.
Yet still, we move through sorrow's heavy veil,
Driven to survive, though parts of us grow frail.

In the ebb and flow of our fleeting ride,
We bear the echoes of each heartache inside.
Though we die in countless, secret ways,
We forge ahead through the dark days.

But in the final dusk of earthly strife,
Beyond the veil of this momentary life,
In the grasp of true death, when we ascend
Our souls will find peace and memories make sense

The fragments we lost find their way to mend,
In the endless cycle where all things blend.
We rise anew, from the ashes of our past,
Embracing eternity, where love infinitely lasts.

8.

In Exile

Like a bird with fractured wings, I flew,
Far from my homeland, where skies were once blue.
Driven by relentless tempests' rage,
I crashed ashore, a ship lost from its stage.

Eager to embrace the dawn of youth,
I arrived with dreams and hope's pursuit.
Yet, my eyes were swiftly veiled,
Unable to behold the beauty unveiled.

Once vibrant eyes, shining with light,
Now dimmed by shadows of endless night.
Longing for my distant shore,
Consumed my heart and soul, and more.

Loneliness, a shadow in my heart,
Springs passed by without their art.
Summer's warmth never kissed my skin,
Flowers withered where dreams had been.

Time, a thief in this alien sphere,
Seized fragments of me year by year.
In exile's frost, I yearn to find
Home's warmth, a love left behind.

9.

My Homeland

Each time I return to you from my travels around the globe
As I watch your green fields from the aeroplane window
I suddenly feel as if my soul reunites with the cosmos
And everything falls into its place

You open your arms to me
As if to console me from the winters of the foreign lands,
Your sun shines brighter than anywhere
Ah, how refreshing, how light is your air

I am recaptured by your smell
So unique, so strong
I feel drunk on your soil
Conquered under your spell

You hold me tight in an embrace
I surrender to your Love
Your warmth, your touch Kosovo my dear,
Fills up all emptiness, melts down my sadness

The voices of my countryman
Are music to my ears
When I walk on your ground
Birds begin to sing

Each time I see the sunset
Disappearing beyond your hills
The red reminds me of the blood
In centuries spilled.

Yet you remain beautiful and heavenly precious
You are a mystery to me, my Kosovo,
My country, my soul, my treasured soil
You may be in pain but never fall.

10.

Beloved mother

Her face, a canvas of the brightest sky,
With loving eyes that inspire, never shy.
Through her, life's meaning becomes clear,
Her presence is a blessing, cherished and dear.

Her smile, a warmth that melts my heart's frost,
In her gaze, I see both pain and strength embossed.
A brave soul, with mesmerising grace,
Winning unseen battles, a model to embrace.

A birthmark, a mark of distinction, so rare,
Her eyes, a source of compassion beyond compare
She stands alone, unique in her tenderness,
Her words are always encouraging, with pure finesse.

With every gesture, she lifts others high,
Her generosity is a gift that will never run dry.
She stands, steadfast, in her tender grace,
Her fountain of wisdom leaves an eternal trace.

A joyful soul, with a heart full of light,
Her strength and love guide me through the darkest night.
Her love, my longing, my world, my guide,
She is my moonlight, my mother, my pride.

A wonderful mother, nurturing and kind,
In her embrace, peace I always find.
She is the core of my love, pure and true,
With her, I am never blue.

Her essence is a light in life's vast sea,
Guiding me home, where my heart longs to be.
Her legacy of love, forever to stay,
In every whispered word and each gentle sway

11.

A Testament to My Daughter

October 15, 2009—a day divine,
A miracle touched this heart of mine.
Untold joy swept through my core,
As you, my angel stepped through life's door.

The day you arrived, my goddess fair,
The heavens opened, love beyond compare.
In God's embrace, with wings unfurled,
I became your guardian, your world.

My soul lit up with love's pure light,
You, sweet innocence, a sacred sight.
The princess of my realm, my best gift in life,
Your joy, my mission in life's flight.

With each year, your radiance grows,
My sweetest daughter, a blossoming rose.
You touch my soul with tender grace,
My inspiration, in every embrace.

May your path be clear, your journey grand,
A star shining bright across the land.
Paint this world with kindness and care,
Be truthful, be brave, and face every dare.

After each trial, learn and grow,
Rise again, let your spirit glow.
Seek the truth, be a guiding light,
For those who wander in the darkest night.

Climb every rainbow, enjoy the chase,
Grow stronger with each love's embrace.
Never forget, to choose love over fear,
Rise, my goddess, with grace sincere.

In your presence, may joy never end,
Wherever you wander, heal and amend.
Draw your dreams, let the music play,
With butterflies dancing, in your pathway.

12.

My Suitcase

In my suitcase, I carry shadows of tears,
The creases of smiles, and laughter through the years.
The hazy shapes of childhood dreams,
Unfinished acts and faded schemes.

My suitcase travels through clouded rays and distant stars,
In the wings of desires, breathless, chasing life's memoirs.
Tracing light while hiding fears,
Pursuing destiny's glory through the years.

Within it, the spirit's essence lies,
Igniting flames where my molecules rise.
Composed of chromosomes, hereditary threads,
Pain, euphoria, triumphs, and truths unsaid.

In a corner, untouched, a pearl remains,
The innocence of a love that never wanes.
A twin-flame dream, a fairy tale unfurled,
Sweet as life itself, yet as bitter as the world.

I carry my suitcase through rainbows' glow,
Etching hieroglyphs where desert winds blow.
I have the Nile, the Danube, and oceans blue,
Their rivers dance within my veins, flowing true.

A suitcase unlocked by the fifth element's key,
Stitched into my soul, in every memory.
My code, my essence, my suitcase within,

Holding first kisses, last tears, life's triumphs and sins.

13.

The Power of Choice

You chose to come to Earth, to learn and to grow,
A soul's mission, written in the stars, is a path to follow.
In life's trials, where challenges ignite,
You're shaped to shine, to step into the light.

Life offers many paths, each door a different fate,
Every choice is a key, to shaping what you create.
So when crossroads appear and fear clouds your view,
Let love be your compass, let your heart's wisdom guide you
through.

In this world of illusions, where paths often split,
Each step is a choice, each decision a shift.
Trust the voice within, let it lead the way,
For your heart knows the truth, come what may.

In every breath, in every turn, lies a choice,
A chance to listen to your inner voice.
Paths diverge in the dance of time,
Each decision shapes your rhythm and rhyme.

When the fog of doubt clouds what's true,
And the mind plays tricks, distorting your view,
Turn to the wisdom that resides within,
Let love, not fear, guide you through to win.

When shadows cast doubt and the road seems unclear,
And the mind weaves tales that breed only fear,
Look within, to the flame that never fades,
Let your soul guide you through life's masquerades.

In the darkest hours, when the burden's too great,
You hold the power to alter your fate.
To give in or rise, to fight or to flee,
Choosing yourself is always the key.

At the crossroads of destiny, where options divide,
Remember your purpose, let your spirit decide.
Leap boldly, even when fear grips tight,
For every test is a spark, a chance to ignite.

You always have a choice, in every breath, every strife,
To shape your destiny, to transform your life.
So choose love, choose light, let your spirit soar,
For in this lifetime, you're here to learn, explore, and love
more.

14.

Life

In the swift current of existence, our days rush by,
A fleeting dream, evaporating into the sky.
Time, an elusive stream, carries all away,
Leaving behind memories, and statues of yesterday.

Warm nights adorned with stars, a memory's embrace,
Springs once blossomed within, a cherished space.
Now, like a river's flow, they vanish in the mist,
Leaving behind the fragrance of flowers once kissed.

Recalling images of the gentle breezes caress,
When the Sun painted warmth, a sweet finesse.
The sky, a canvas bending with ideals so grand,
Now echoes the cry of the moon, a destiny unplanned.

Summoning visions of the soft breeze's touch,
As the Sun bestowed its warmth, a sweet clutch.
The sky, a canvas with ideals so grand,
Now resonates with the moon's unforeseen command.

Inevitable destinies whisper in the moonlit night,
Time hastens its pace in our transient flight.
Shadows we become in this celestial journey,
Our traces were lost to the wind, in a brief passage.

15.

True Friendship

Through each stage of life, in every age,
I've met many people along the way,
Yet only a few have truly remained,
True jewels in my stardom, forever ingrained.

One of life's blessings, a precious gift,
Is a friend who understands, without a rift.
A companion who needs no explanation,
Their presence alone brings sweet elation.

This friend walks with you through storm and light,
Lifting you up when all seems night.
With them, laughter is pure and free,
In their company, you're never lonely.

Together you share both joy and sorrow,
This bond, sacred, grows with each tomorrow.
True friendship is earned and carved deep within,
As the years pass by, through thick and thin.

You become each other's strength and guide,
Inspiring one another to rise and thrive.
Of all the blessings with priceless cost
It's my friendships that I cherish most.

For a true friend is loyal, steadfast, and true,
Someone you trust with all that's you.
Through battles fought and victories won,
They stand by your side, your constant sun.

In every game, in loss or gain,
They bring you joy, easing your pain.
Reminding you of who you are,
Accepting you fully, near or far.

Sharing secrets, dreams, and fears,
A true friend is with you through the years.
In this sacred bond, so rare and fine,
I'm grateful for the friendship that's forever mine.

16.

Mission

Embarking on each day with the sun's golden light,
Inhaling the essence of summer, pure and bright.
Greeting the sky with wings that soar and sing,
Touching the sea where echoes softly ring.

Always embracing others with boundless love,
Enriching my soul with kindness from above.
Tenderly navigating each space to ease the pain,
With clear insight, crafting life's vibrant terrain.

Guided by wisdom to console weary hearts,
Ingrain time with immortal arts.
Believing in miracles, making them true,
Healing the world from its veil of blue.

17.

Drowsing between dreams

With heavy lids, I drift through dreamland's gate,
Bathed in visions that softly captivate.
How vivid, how unreal,
How close, how distant, yet surreal.

Like echoes from the mountain's crest,
I carry the world's weight in my silent quest,
In every breath, I claim my part,
For all that exists beats in my heart.

I am not just a fragment of the cosmic sea;
I am the universe, expansive and free.
I'm not a mere part of cosmic design;
I am the heavens themselves, vast and divine.

No thrill from stars in their celestial dance,
I am the tear's essence, the light in the glance,
The flame of the soul, burning bright and pure,
Intoxicated by love that's eternal and sure.

I drift forever through dreams and hope's embrace,
An angel, a light, in boundless space.
In this epiphany, my soul's true sight,
Reveals not mere flesh, but star-born light.

18.

Epiphany

Tonight, she uncovered the mystery,
A divine message, sudden and serene.
Shadows fled, clouds evaporated,
The sky opened with a radiant beam.

Tonight, everything turned into pure delight,
A moment of awakening, so bright.
Earthly illusions can no longer withhold
The treasure within like the most precious gold,

Once her vision was clouded, now crystal clear,
Seeing beyond every veil, without fear.
Climbing without wings, hearing every sound,
Revelations in whispers, profound.

Signs screamed in synchronicity,
Clear as daylight, embodying them within diligently
Inside her dreams, angelic voices,
"Be bold, do not fear, trust your choices."

Ships in undocked ports began to sway,
Dancing lightly with the playful breeze.
An invitation to set sail, to seize the day,
The old map now led to hidden keys.

In dark caves, she ventured alone,
Discovering diamonds, her courage had grown.
With dragons, she fought, fierce and unyielding,
Overcoming battles, her spirit revealing.

Tonight, she felt more alive than ever,
Like a divine being, limitless in power.
Returning to the tranquillity of inner waters,
Embracing the fruits of her journey, she found her core.

She is alive, she is divine, she is herself again,
A wanderer of her destiny, beyond mortal pain.
Essence and energy, everything and nothing,
Unveiling divine truth, the secret of living.

Under the reign of waterfalls,
Guided by stars high above,
She understands she is the captain of her fate,
The power within can unlock every gate.

In the depths of her soul's sacred space,
Divine purpose shines with gentle grace.
A wanderer with a destined role,
Unveiling her truth, as she seeks her soul.

19.

Riverside Prayer

In the early mornings by the river's side,
Awaiting the sun, our hearts open wide.
As daylight dawns, a collective sigh we send,
Welcoming the new day, may its brilliance never end.

How many tears, how much light bestowed?
As the river and I along its currents flowed?
Infused with hope, a ritual prayer we share,
Believing in miracles, breathing in the air.

Beneath the open sky, we gracefully bow,
Seeking a piece of sun, a sprinkle of rain, somehow.
The furious river, a force within my veins,
Carries eagles aloft, releasing nostalgic strains.

Each wave tells tales, an untold story,
From my spring source to where waves merge in glory.
Bits of history, mystical symbols in flow,
Crowned and withered flowers, the river does bestow.

My journey continues, an endless dance,
To the rhythm of the night, a starlit trance.
By the purity of dawn, I seek a touch of wonder,
A bittersweet memory where joy and sorrow ponder.

Let me dip gently into your waters, divine,
Quenching my thirst in your embrace is so fine.
As laughter echoes, Death seals holy paths,
A prayer along the river, embracing life's aftermath.

20.

The Journey

I walked through the fields of gold,
On a journey long and cold,
With nothing but my dreams to hold,
And the memories of stories told.

I followed the path where the wind would bend,
Through forests, valleys, and mountains' end,
Crossing rivers and meandering streams,
Chasing echoes of distant dreams.

The sun would rise and softly fall,
As I continued through it all,
Through joy and dismay, I'd stand tall,
Holding my head high, I would not stall.

With each step, the past was cast aside,
In search of a world where dreams abide,
Filled with wonder, beauty unrefined,
And a love that I could claim as mine.

As the days turned into weeks,
I found myself climbing peaks,
And crossing treacherous creeks,
But my spirit never grew weak.

For the journey taught me all I need,
Strength and courage were my creed,
With every step, I sowed the seed,
Of wisdom's quiet, gentle lead.

And now, as I near journey's end,
I look back on the road I've been,
And see the beauty in every scene,
I know my soul will forever be serene.

21.

Unwritten Sorrows

So many times, I've wished for strength,
To write the longest poem, at length.
To melt my soul's pain into every line,
But my hand stays frozen, refusing to sign

Unable to capture what my heart feels within…
Perhaps it dreads the storm of deep-seated pain,
Tears streaming in a boundless flow,
Urging to heal through words, to grow.

Each line of this poem, a tale of sorrow,
Revealing grief that seeks to borrow
Yearning for release, a cry from the past,
Unveiling the turmoil within my soul at last.

With words, I mend my heart's deep wound,
In resilience and strength, my spirit is found.
Through writing's therapeutic art,
Enlightenment blooms from life's painful part.

22.

From Ashes to Light

Enchanted, she flutters in déjà vu,
A violet dream tinged with rainbow hue,
A silent mystery, without a hint or clue,
Life's trials with a bitter taste,
Embers of fire shimmer, extinguished, lost, and erased.

A vision with wings through sins does soar,
Thirst's origin from the cosmos's core,
On her back, a sack of Egyptian sand,
Holding pyramids in her hand,
Wingless, she ascends to the celestial sphere,
Touching stars, the moon, and the sun.

With the sixth sense, since she's been on Mars,
Bones starved, nourished by blood's red waterfall,
Human essence flowing through her veins,
Kissing stars in the galaxy, for love alone,
She'll resurrect, recreate, and sacrifice once more.

A surge of energy still thunders,
A light extinguished, awaiting rebirth,
A withered flower prays with a voice soft and sore,
Before the Almighty, like a white rose, she bows

From ruins, she is raised, given breath, sun and life.
Reborn in dimensions of crystal waters,
Earth will become her feathered bed,
Together, dancing tango within her mind, body and soul
Spirit, tears, and love will entwine,
She'll never lose faith, forever believe in the Divine.

23.

Positive vibes

In the realm of positivity where life's tales unfold,
A gentle reminder, a beacon to behold
In the canvas of your days, paint tints of thanks,
A gratitude journal, where each moment ranks.

Simple joys, like a shared dinner delight,
Illuminate your world, turning darkness into light.
Share your time, a treasure so divine,
Give, and watch the universe align.

Tithe to causes with compassion's thread,
Weave connections where empathy is spread.
Acts so random, like stars in the night,
Brighten hearts, spreading pure delight.

The giver and receiver in harmony sway,
A dance of kindness in life's grand ballet.
Be the captain of your destiny's ship,
No victimhood here, no blame to grip.

Reclaim your power, let positivity grow,
Plant it deep within, let your soul's light show.
Don't sweat the small stuff, for it's all but tiny,
Transient moments, passing and shiny.

Know that bad times are but a fleeting gust,
Seeds for future blessings, in which we trust.
Hold these truths close, let them be your guide,
Watch as positive changes in your life reside.

In gratitude, kindness, and empathy,
Life's symphony plays a harmonious melody.
With every step, let your heart remain true,
And the light you share will always renew.

24.

Photograph of My Past

A face now marked by storms of the soul,
Eyes once radiant, now strangers to their role.
"Do you recognize her?" they ask of me,
I answer, "Only shadows of who I used to be."

In the mirror of time, I seek my past's grace,
Was that truly me, adorned in life's embrace?
Were those eyes once ablaze with passion's fire,
Yearning not just for love, but for my own heart's desire?

I study the photograph, or does it study me?
A silent witness to the mysteries of destiny.
"What have you become?" it seems to accuse,
And I reply, "You never foresaw the path I'd choose."

In the photograph's frame, my past self-stares,
"What have you transformed into?" it quietly inquires,
Yet from the ashes, I rise anew,
Bearing the scars, but with a clearer view."

25.

I Wish

To have faith and chase dreams untamed
To find strength within and live truth unashamed
Amidst life's trials, to love without fear,
To recall the purity of my essence, so dear,
When I was just a free wandering soul,

I wish I could show you the vision I see,
Your enchanting soul, unchained and free.
You are stardust, a miracle in bloom,
Freed from the shackles of this earthly gloom.

I wish I could express the love I hold,
A tapestry of feelings, rich and bold.
I wish I could paint the sorrow and pain,
In colours that endure, despite the strain.

I wish I could show how I've yearned to breathe free,
I wish I didn't have to wear strength for the world to see,
Or hide my tears with a smile, while my heart silently weeps.
I wish I could love unconditionally, with a heart that freely leaps.

Path To Love

1.

Secret Passion

Where can I cast this blazing fire,
The passion within me, my heart's desire?
Whom shall I take to the heights of bliss,
And share with them my purest kiss?

Who will embrace my innocent soul,
And cherish the dreams that make me whole?
Is there a soul that mirrors mine,
Who knows my depths without a sign?

In silent moments, side by side,
Loving me truly, with nothing to hide.
Whose shoulder will cradle my weary head,
What scent will soothe when hope has fled?

Who will light the path when the night is long,
And hold me close until the dawn?
For whom shall I burn like a star in the sky,
And with my final breath, who will I kiss goodbye?

2.

In Love's Pure Light

Hope one day we shall meet again,
In a realm untouched by pain,
Where souls unchained find sweet release,
From this world's torment, into boundless peace.

No need for remorse, nor foolish pride,
Only souls that gently collide,
Where love alone will win the race,
And every scar finds healing grace.

I crave to see you, pure and clear,
With eyes that are freed from the blindness of fear,
A heart that's healed, forever free,
Rejoicing in love's purest decree.

In the other world, we shine as stars,
Free from the burden of earthly scars,
Freely fluttering in the universe,
Without tears, bitterness, or greed
Only you, love, and I.

We'll dance and laugh in perfect harmony,
As angels bathe us in light's pure symphony.
From up above, the world will appear anew,
Yet all that matters is being beside you.

I yearn to kiss you with love so true,
As parched lips melt in tender dew,
A passion that whispers soft and deep,
Where love is the language our souls speak.

3.

Loneliness

Loneliness, why do you summon these tears,
A chilling breeze that halts the flower's bloom?
Why must you press with such heavyweight,
And bring silent pain to the soul's quiet room?

Within the prison walls, feelings wilt away,
No visitor comes to bring them light or stay.
Darkness, aching for a spark to ignite,
Bearing the weight of pain, leaving light breathless in the night.

Why do tears companion every passing day,
The broken heart dreads each breath it takes.
Nights unfold with dreams draped in despair,
Loneliness is an unwelcome companion we bear.

Loneliness, why conjure tears so deep,
As the cold breeze envelopes, the flowers sleep.
Why weigh so heavily with an ache profound,
Punishing the soul in silence, without sound?

Why do countless tears fall with each passing day?
A broken heart fears to breathe, lest joy decay?
The nights unfold with dreams steeped in despair,
Yet within, a glimmer of hope clings to the air.

Heavy is the burden, but from shadows, strength will rise,
Turning tears into pearls, a soul's hard-earned prize.
Loneliness, in your grasp, an evolution takes flight,
Where pain transforms into an unforeseen, resilient light.

4.

Sea's Serenade

Above the seaside sky, stars shine bright,
The moon softly laughs, with tender light.
Waves embrace the rocks in secret tryst,
Just as lovers in the night's gentle mist.
.

Each breeze flows through my veins with ease,
A rhythmic dance that brings me peace.
With spirit and universe perfectly aligned,
Tonight, I long to be a wave, unconfined.

Eternally part of the sea's mystic grave.
Never again to feel alone,
Nor for my eyes to weep or groan,
Or my heart to shudder from hidden pain.

I wish to be like waves, wild and free,
Bound to the sea's eternal symphony.
In the moonlight's dance, where spirits merge,
I long to drift where the tides converge.

5.

June's Enchanted Shore

On a warm June night, the breeze soft and kind,
Strolling by the sea, on Cyprus' shore I find.
Moon and stars cast a divine glow,
Whispers of waves, like sweet wine's flow.

Alone with my dreams, I traverse the sand,
Your face is in my mind, my heart takes a stand.
The sea's scent intoxicates me like your embrace,
I'm lost in this beauty, in a tranquil space.

My footsteps fade into the darkened shore,
The white waves continue their timeless lore.
With each step, memories dance in the night,
Under the canopy of stars, bathed in their light.

6.

Rain in Pristina

Lightning storms and torrential rain,
I walk Pristina's streets again,
Without an umbrella, I embrace the night,
Kissing the rain with pure delight.

Darkness wraps the city's sky,
As the rain continues, I'm left awry,
Enchanted by the night's mystique,
Life's fragrance in the air is so sweet.

The sky unleashes its fierce embrace,
Flashing over the earth's dry face,
Intoxicated by lightning's spark,
I feel the storm ignite my heart.

Rain keeps falling, I'm spellbound,
Each drop a whisper, each sound profound,
Adrift in life's relentless wave,
Yet thirsting for the storm's fierce crave.

Like lightning striking, hope's faint gleam,
Brightens within, a distant dream,
I feel the storm within my chest,
In Pristina's night, I'm truly blessed.

I merge with wind, with rain, with sky,
This magic night, I can't deny,
In Pristina's arms, I find my place,
Enchanted by the storm's embrace.

7.

Regret

Often you visit me in dreams,
Disturbing my sleep's serene streams.
Your face faded, worn and pale,
Reveals the weight of your remorseful tale.

In dreams, your hands reach through the mist,
Calling my name, a distant twist.
I see the tear that graces your eye,
And the ache that your heart cannot deny.

Please, leave my dreams to their gentle rest,
Follow your path where fate has pressed.
Regret arrives when it's too late,
You've broken my spirit, sealed our fate.

Let me find peace in dreams' gentle arms,
Perhaps the sun's warmth may offer its charms.
Love has withered, its petals torn away
Now I chose my own destined way

8.

Unchained Heart

You are no longer the star that lights my sky,
No longer the wound where my youthful dreams lie.
Your name, once cherished, fades without a trace,
And your love, a shadow, leaves an empty space.

Your face, now a phantom, dims in my sight,
I no longer see you in the soft glow of night.
Your touch and your voice, now distant and cold,
I no longer know you; your story's been told.

You carry the weight of a grand, hollow lie,
An extinguished flame beneath an empty sky.
The dust of false promises, swept by the storm,
Snuffed out the lamp that once kept me warm.

For me, the vibrant paintings have turned grey,
The melody of your guitar fades away.
Your words, once magic, now fall to the floor,
All that was yours, for me, is no more.

I see the truth now, clear and stark,
You were never the love that lit up my dark.
An illusion shattered, a dream turned to ash,
Leaving emptiness where once was a flash.

In this moment of clarity, I finally see,
The chains have been broken; my heart set free.
With indifference awakened, I make a new start,
For now, I possess an unchained heart.

9.

Lesson learned

To love amidst the storm of hate,
To smile through tears that resonate,
To give when your own need is dire,
Swallow pride, with grace, aspire.

Close your eyes to harsh truths that sting,
Pretend deaf to voices that loudly ring.
In love's game, rules are elusive as mist,
A fragile tie that barely exists.

Near yet far, breathing the same air,
Worlds apart, like stars in a flare.
No code to decipher, no formula set,
Love's struggle is eternal, a constant bet.

Each story is unique, like sands on the shore,
With varied ingredients, tales to explore.
Yet give love when hope seems lost,
and lead them gently through the frost.

Be authentic, radiant and bright,
Love not for return, but to be hope's light.
To guide the lost, in their deepest despair,
In love's darkest hour, always be there.

Expecting nothing, no strings or conditions,
To love is the lesson, in life's true mission.
In bloodshed of tears, in heartbreak's song,
To love is to learn, to remain strong.

10.

In Love with the World

A snowy night, the world aglow,
Candlelight flickers, warming the soul.
Let the cold winds blow, for I am warmed,
By the smile of a dream, pure and adorned.

I see love in the sparkle of your eyes,
Kicking fear into its shadowed lies
I gaze into love's welcoming embrace,
Throwing open the gates, I call it with grace.

We play with snowflakes in a joyful spree,
Like children lost in playful glee.
The sky was our shelter, snow pure and white,
The earth is our bed, as soft as feathered light.

In secret, we kiss with passionate fire,
Above the snow, we dance in desire.
In this moment, hearts unfrozen, free,
In love with the world, just you and me.

11.

Awaiting

Rain taps softly on my window glass,
Clock hands crawl as moments pass.
My heart beats frantic, filled with despair,
Awaiting a call, a heartbreak to repair.

The phone remains silent, offering no peace,
Hope fades after a long and fruitless wait.
Centuries seem to pass in yearning that thrills,
Yet nothing stirs, just a stillness that kills.

Tears fall gently over the phone,
Echoes of distance carve a wall of stone.
Desire burns with a fevered flame,
Just for a moment, I lean into love's name.

Sweet memories linger, tender and kind,
Are they real or just illusions in my mind?
Loneliness echoes with the rain's soft cry,
Yet, I wait beneath this weeping sky.

I can't believe it, I can't let it go,
Suddenly it dawns on me, slow.
Craving whispers through the rain's refrain,
And I endure this silent, aching pain.

12.

The Long Wait for Love

Amidst the celestial dance of countless starlit nights,
To the rhythm of summer's soft, inviting lights,
The sea's lingering scent whispered tales untold,
On a canvas where my prayers for you were gently scrolled.

Silent cries echoed within the chambers of my heart,
Longing for the other half, a puzzle torn apart.
My tears, like tributaries, joined the vast seas,
Each drop is a testament to desires, carried by the summer breeze.

Yearning, a force so potent and intense,
My heart, overwhelmed, built walls in self-defence.
Gates closed, and loneliness became my guest,
A sanctuary of solitude, where in longing, I'm dressed.

Loneliness, a silent companion, embraced my soul,
A tale of waiting, love's story yet to unfold.
Divine timing waits for destinies to align,
But now my soul whispers, it's my time.

13.

Unexpected

When destiny whispers, you have no clue,
A day like any other, yet something new,
An inner force propels you toward the unknown,
surprising excitement inside your very core.

An unexpected knock upon your soul's door,
Embracing nightfall's unforeseen allure.
Not realizing this knock could break or bestow,
Showering love's sweet light into your soul.

There are no incidents in the universal realm,
truly everything is orchestrated in harmony...
an ordinary night on earth-
it's staged by angels in perfect synchronicity.

One sacred moment, one holy night,
Touches your heart with unexpected light.
Longing souls meet, stars align above,
Written in constellations, fate's grand love.

A joyful reunion leaves you craving more,
Soul enveloped in warmth to its core.
Is this love's true form or a twist of fate?
A game of Destiny or Forever's Gate?

Innocent moments, hearts miss a beat,
Longing for another soul, sweet and complete.
Cells dance in rhythm, unexpectedly aligned,
In the sweet embrace of love's design.

14.

Destined Encounter

One lucky night, as the concert's final chord was played,
You embraced me like a long-lost friend.
In that moment, our souls intertwined,
Bound by a tie we couldn't comprehend.

Years apart, yet suddenly so near,
An unexpected spark, a flame so clear.
Our paths crossed by destiny's design,
A magical moment, beautifully divine.

Your warmth melted my frozen heart,
My soul found its mirror, a perfect part,
Something happened, beyond what words can say,
An enchantment that took our breaths away.

Yet fate's lessons can be harsh and severe,
In the glow of love, we sometimes burn.
Even if our paths diverge, our hearts remain,
Forever touched by this unforgettable flame.

We must cherish the magic, the moments we've known,
Appreciate the love that in our hearts has grown.
For even if together we may not stay,
Our bond's essence will forever play.

Let's learn from this, embrace the light,
Keep each other close, in the quiet of the night.
In our hearts, this memory will forever reside,
A testament to a love that time cannot divide.

15.

The Distance

In my depths, your absence echoes loud,
Your light within, a radiant cloud,
Your essence fills my lungs, each breath,
Your warmth, a melody, defying death.

Sweet whispers linger, close and near,
Your presence craved, your smile so dear,
With each waking moment, you're in sight,
Yet distance separates, dimming the light.

Your heart's ache resonates deep in my core,
Drawn to you, craving more and more,
Your scent lingers, a tantalizing trace,
Without you, stars fade, leaving empty space.

Colours come alive within your embrace,
Craving to hold you, feel your grace,
Every part of you, I yearn to explore,
Distance fuels our love, begging for more.

I burn to ignite you, atom by atom,
To taste your lips, in passion's fathom,
In our fiery union, we're born anew,
Yet in this distance, my heart aches for you.

16.

Echoes of Wishes

As you wish, a voice profound,
Concealing pain where whispers drown.
In silence, I softly confess,
Wishing as snow's gentle caress.

I yearn to see your unguarded skin,
Bare and pure, free from shadows within.
To unchain you from your self-made plight,
And let your light dance in the night.

A smile in your wondering eyes, I desire,
With my foolishness, a naked heart is on fire.
To soar to the sky, on wings untold,
Reveal the rainbow's hues, a spectacle to behold.

A mirror to show your own magnificence,
Painted with the magic of innocence.
To replace your pain, erase your fear,
Hold you close, yet set you free, my dear.

Silently, I wish to whisper to your soul,
Be yourself, and let your heart unroll.
As I wish, as you wish, echoes entwine,
In the realm of wishes, our destinies align.

17.

You and Me

You and I, two facets of the same coin,
Halves of each other, longing to re-join.
Cracked, burning lips yearning for that kiss,
Broken hearts aching from what we miss.

We exist in thought, not yet in this reality,
Eloped in the ecstasy of eternal memory.
Recognizing each other, feeding from shared energy,
Our love is imprinted deep within our divinity.

In the higher realms, our love ignites,
A most passionate affair, beyond earthly sights.
This soul connection, so strong, so unique,
Feels like yearning for love in despair's peak.

Cruel lessons, we both have endured,
Searching for each other through the earthly veil, obscured.
To evolve, to renew our soul's sacred pact,
Earthly trials may bend but never crack.

Amidst the thickest fog, the darkest night,
I knew your aura, I recognized your soul light
And it was all worth it, to love you once more,
To rekindle the flame, we shared before.

18.

Bound by destiny

It's been months since the shadows
Of a broken heart shattered my light,
Countless moments passed in time,
Yet, your face lingers in the corridors of my mind.

Far in distance, yet intimately close,
Silently suffering the twists of fate's prose.
I set you free, granted you wings to soar,
While I remained tethered, waiting evermore.

In the hush of nights, I struggled to release,
To sever the ties that bound us, seeking peace.
Yet, in the quiet echoes of my own soul,
I discovered traces of you, making me whole.

I distanced myself from the core within,
Hoping you'll find your path, and where to begin.
Yet, you lingered stubbornly, an ethereal part,
Entwined in the fabric of my beating heart.

Then, a day arrived, clouds cleared away,
Blue skies returned, in a celestial display.
You and I, bound by a destiny untold,
No shadows too dark for our love to unfold.

19.

Divine Gift

I wonder why I love you, from that first glance,
Your eyes met mine in a cosmic dance.
My heart knew yours, a spark so bright,
Since we met, everything feels so right.

It's like a dream where only we exist,
Lost in each other's energy, an eternal twist.
Amid earthly chatter, we find our calm,
As words fade away in love's tender charm.

One touch ignites a fire, souls intertwined,
In your presence, inspiration finds its bind.
No logic explains this deep connection's flight,
Yet it's the most beautiful truth in plain sight.

Feeling you near, I'm lifted to my peak,
Living fully, your love makes me strong and meek.
It's a journey where you inspire, motivate,
Guiding me to heights, my destined fate.

I want to freeze this moment, hold you tight,
You're my soul's compass, my guiding light.
Meant to be, a love so uniquely true,
A gift from the stars, I found in you.

20.

Love and Fear

Stop—I feel you from afar,
Your troubled soul, your hidden scar.
I've touched you deeply, reached your core,
In ways you've never felt before.

You yearn for me, you question why,
Without me, a part of you seems to die.
Why do you feel less without me near?
Why does my absence spark such fear?

How can one night, one gentle touch,
Awaken such longing, stir you so much?
Sweet and sour feelings, confusion's sting,
Paralysing fears of what love might bring.

I sense the emptiness in your heart,
Coldness grips you as if I've stolen the sun's warmth.
The air has lost its sweetness, every song a haunting tune,
Echoes of love stir your soul beneath the moon.

In the depths of your soul, fear hides and coils,
Yet your spirit betrays, as love unravels the toils.
Your heart surrenders where love quietly lies,
You're less of yourself but more of us, you realise.

In love's embrace, there's no need to rush,
Though fear may whisper and doubts may fuss,
Our hearts beat together, in unity and trust,
In this shared love, we find what's just.

You wonder what this love could be,
Choosing to flee rather than see,
Yet fighting it only makes love prevail,
I feel you from the distance, beyond the veil.

21.

Purple Fields of Love

You can truly love, once you walk the truth's path,
Within its rainbow colours, that cleanses all wrath
Showered in a waterfall that washes away all sins
And buries traces of ego deep within.

A parched soul finds unity's embrace,
After passing through the earthly illusion's gates,
Breaking shadows, reaching for light,
Embodying truth in a fusion so bright.

One breathes freely, reborn in magnificence,
Freed and revived in love's pure essence.
Rejoicing in the wonders of purple fields,
After journeying through the soul's dark yields.

Paradise's warmth is felt within,
When love flows in eternity's stream.
Crossing fear's fire, ascending to grace,
In love's energy, we find our place.

To master this timeless, universal game,
Unite with the soul in a cosmic flame.
Transcend into stardust, evolve with ease,
Become the highest frequency breeze.

22.

Cosmic Tango

In twilight's quiet, truths unfold,
Revealing secrets where shadows once controlled.
We were broken, lost in life's storm,
But now our souls, together, warm.

Illusion's fade, barriers fall,
Silent voices rise, answering love's call.
Fate's threads weave a timeless bond,
Two hearts beat as one, beyond and beyond.

A dance of souls, yearning to be whole,
In this truth, our love takes hold.
Two halves of a cosmic embrace,
Together we heal in love's sacred space.

From earthly bounds to celestial flight,
Guiding others towards the light.
Our journey, the soul's deepest goal,
Together we flourish, becoming whole

In love's triumph, we find our grace,
Spreading light in this sacred place.
Evolving, ascending, in soul's delight,
Dancing forever in cosmic light.

23.

Perfect Symphony

Two souls bound in a karmic dance,
Reflecting wounds with every glance.
Illuminating shadows from the past,
Desperate to ignite the light at last.

A journey powerful yet soul-breaking,
Magnetic pull, with hearts aching.
To find peace and love within,
Why must we walk through fire to begin?

A divine plan, an inescapable fate,
Even when we tried to deviate.
It's hard to grasp this love so rare,
Pretending it exists only in dreams' air.

Love so obsessive, fiercely strong,
Driving us mad, desperate and long.
Our wounded hearts struggle to understand,
Yet your existence gives me strength to withstand.

This world, with its relentless twists,
Feels mundane, lost in foggy mists.
Why traverse this lifetime's span,
Only to meet, to learn again?

I crave a shortcut to your embrace,
To surrender to love in your sacred space.
Tired of waiting, trials exhaust,
Yet I learn new love's true cost.

The mirror and candle you hold so high,
Reveal my shadows, gently pry.
Through tunnels of strength, I discover,
A journey to love, to self-recover.

You pressed my buttons, I pressed yours,
Yet all I wished was to heal your sores.
To ease your pain, to lift the veil,
So, you could see your divinity prevail.

You, the brightest star in my sky,
My only true love, my live or die.
Let's brave this gift, divinely sent,
To fulfil our purpose, to love, to ascend.

Courage to endure, to embrace,
The path that leads to our rightful place.
Back to our soul's mission, pure and grand,
To love you, me, and us, hand in hand.

Understanding our purpose, we must align,
Dancing to our soul's music, by design.
Captivated by divinity's perfect symphony,
In this dance, we're destined for eternity.

24.

Surrender

When your dream gets shattered into millions of pieces,
When your heart breaks and you can't breathe
When you witness the hopes suddenly disappear
Take a step back and surrender

Feel the pain, sharp as a blade,
Embrace the end; with the grief become a friend
When emptiness and apathy are all that's left,
Surrender to the universe, have complete faith

Face the fear of a future unknown,
Impossible destinies love overthrown.
Remember to surrender to fate's decree,
What's meant for you will always be.

Surrender to destiny's mysterious path,
Maybe a Brighter future is written for you in the stars
Let go of loss, pain, and despair-release the past
Have faith, choose a new beginning, and be ready for a blast.

25.

"Why I Write"?

I write because my essence yearns to speak,
Breathing life into words, on the page I seek.
Ink flows from the pen, a dance of soul and thought,
A sacred craft, from which I cannot be distraught.

I write to feel the thunder, the sun's embrace,
To taste the rain and every tear's trace.
Each word a vessel, carrying my heart's song,
In joy, in sorrow, in life's ever-long.

I write to witness life's miracles unfold,
To share with others, both young and old.
Drinking deep from the well of shared humanity,
Finding solace, joy, in words' infinity.

In laughter, in tears, in every twist of fate,
I find my refuge in the stories I create.
For I am the writer, bound to this sacred art,
With each stroke of the pen, I reveal my heart's part,

9 789364 523240